VILLAGE TOWN, CITY

Written by
John Corn

Illustrated by
Hardlines, Steve Noon, Emma Whiting

Edited by
Christina Digby

Designed by
Peter Shirtcliffe

Picture research by
Deirdre O'Day

CONTENTS

Heads or tails	2	Environmental change - villages	26
What is a settlement?	4	Land use in towns	28
Settlement types	6	Places change	30
Home from home	8	Out-of-town shopping	32
Contrasts - New York City	10	Bypass	34
Contrasts - villages in Pakistan	12	Journey through a city	36
Contrasts - Rio de Janiero	14	City centres	38
How it all began	16	Houses in the United Kingdom	40
Early settlements	18	Transport - too much	42
East Morton	20	Environmental change - cities	44
Shops and shopping	22	Conurbations	46
Transport - too little	24	Index	48

2 Heads or tails

There are many things that make us happy or sad. For adults it may be going to work, paying bills or having a brand new car. For children, it may be playing with friends, doing homework or watching a favourite football team win. The place we live in can also affect our moods.

Some people prefer to live in a busy town. They want to be surrounded by people and things to do, so they overlook all the bad things. Other people prefer a slower, quieter pace of life, in a place where it is often easier to get to know people. What do you think?

There are good and bad things about living in villages, towns and cities. The view we have about them depends on many things: whether we are old or young, have a car or not, whether we prefer peace and quiet to noise and bustle. The chances are that at some time in our lives we will have the chance to live in one or other of them - maybe even both.

4 What are settlements?

Settlements are places where people live. Settlements are different shapes and sizes. They may be very small, like farms and hamlets, or very big, like towns and cities. The bigger the settlement, the greater the number and variety of homes.

In large settlements there are a lot of flats and terraced houses. In villages there are more farm houses and cottages, which are rarely seen in towns or cities.

High rise flats

Thatched cottage

Farm

Mobile home

Modern semi-detached house

Large Victorian detached house

Terraced houses

Bungalow

No matter what kind of home you live in, it is probably similar to one of these. Some houses are big, others are small. Some have gardens, others do not, but they are all found in settlements.

Settlement types

There is a variety of types and sizes of settlements. The smallest are farms, the largest are cities such as London, Birmingham, Glasgow and Belfast. There are thousands of farms, each one being home to just a few people. There are only a few cities, but each one is home to hundreds of thousands, even millions, of people. In between are hamlets, villages and towns.

Farms are usually home to only a few people. They are found in the countryside away from other settlements.

Hamlets have populations of between 10 and 100 people in a small group of houses. They have very few services, perhaps a telephone kiosk and a post box. Some hamlets have a public house.

Villages are larger settlements and may have populations of between 100 and 5000 people. They have a number of services including some small shops, a village hall, a church, a post office, a bus stop and a primary school.

UK settlements

- The oldest town in the United Kingdom is believed to be Colchester.

- The remotest village is Inverie in Scotland. It is over 40 kilometres from its nearest neighbour.

- The smallest settlement to have a town council is Fordwich in Kent. It has a population of 249!

Cities are very complex settlements and may have populations of millions. They can offer all types of services, including colleges, cathedrals, museums, art galleries and airports.

Towns are quite complex settlements with populations of up to about 200 000 people. They have a wide range of services which usually includes libraries, secondary schools, bus and railway stations, supermarkets, department stores and police stations.

The larger the settlement, the more services, shops, schools, libraries and hospitals it can offer. Towns and cities provide services which people who live in them or nearby can use. They may be centres for local newspapers, radio stations and entertainment. People might be sent out from towns and cities to repair washing machines or deliver furniture.

8 Home from home

Most settlements have grown steadily from small villages, but not all. Some have been specially built over just a few years.

Purpose-built settlements are not a new idea. Sir Titus Salt, a Victorian mill owner from Yorkshire, built an entire village for his workers. He wanted his workers to live near the mill so that they would not be late for work. Also, he was shocked by the dreadful condition of nearby houses which were little more than slums. His village was called Saltaire, named both after Sir Titus and the river that runs next to it, the Aire. In the village was a hospital, a wash house, alms houses for the elderly, and a park. He provided his workers with a standard of living that was almost unheard of among poor people.

Workers' houses in Saltaire

In 1946 the government decided to build a number of new towns near large cities. The idea was that these towns would help to reduce overcrowding in the cities and stop them spreading. The new towns would also give people new houses to live in, with gardens.

Houses by a canal in Milton Keynes

New towns
- Over 30 new towns have been planned and built since the Second World War.
- One of the largest, Milton Keynes, has a population of 200 000 people.
- At the height of building in the town, 16 500 houses were built in one year.

Billy Butlin wanted to give holidaymakers a new kind of holiday. He wanted to give them the freedom to do what they wanted, and to enjoy lots of different kinds of entertainment. He built chalet homes for people to live in for the week or two that they were on holiday. His first holiday camp opened in Skegness in Lincolnshire in 1936. It was so popular that other holiday camps followed in England, Wales and Scotland. Holiday villages based on his idea are now common on the coast, with rows of mobile homes parked around a central leisure complex.

Butlin's camp, Skegness, 1950s

A modern holiday village in Northumbria

Other settlements have been planned for different reasons. Glenrothes in Scotland was built to house workers near a new colliery; Corby in Northamptonshire grew around a giant steelworks. In 1995 the people of a mining village called Arkwright, in Derbyshire, began to move into a brand new, purpose-built village less than one kilometre away. This was because methane gas was escaping into the old village from rocks below.

Contrasts – New York City

Manhattan skyline from the Hudson River

The 'Big Apple', as New York City is sometimes called, is to many people the most thrilling city in the world. It is full of sights and sounds very different to any city in the United Kingdom.

Most people imagine New York as a city full of skyscrapers. In one part of New York, Manhattan, this is true. Manhattan is an island twenty kilometres long and just three kilometres wide. It has a towering skyline which includes some of the tallest buildings in the world, such as the twin towers of the World Trade Centre and the Empire State Building. The other districts which make up New York City are Brooklyn, the Bronx, Queens, and Staten Island.

The layout of roads in Manhattan is very organised. Avenues run north to south, while streets run east to west. Between them are blocks: high rise buildings of shops, offices or hotels. Macys, one of the largest stores in the world, takes up one whole block and is many stories high. The layout of roads in New York makes it difficult to get lost if you are walking. You simply count as you pass each numbered street. Driving is a different matter.

New York City
- New York is the largest city in the United States of America.
- It has a population of 7.3 million people.
- Each year about 20 million people visit the city.
- The World Trade Centre buildings are 420 metres high - almost twice as tall as the Canary Wharf Tower in London.

New York City has thousands of kilometres of road but travelling on them can be a nightmare. Driving is often the slowest way to get anywhere. Most New Yorkers use the subway, much of which is overground, or trains if they live further away. Yellow cabs are a common sight on the roads. They are quite cheap and used by most people - but it is not easy to catch one!

One and a half million people live on Manhattan, mostly in the centre and the north. People of different cultures have chosen to live in some districts, such as Chinatown, Little Italy and Harlem. Greenwich Village is the home of many artists and writers. It has many restaurants and craft shops.

Yellow taxi cabs in New York

New York is full of places to visit. Central Park in Manhattan is about 3.5 square kilometres. Here people jog, rollerblade, picnic or gently tour the Park in a pony and trap. From Battery Park a ferry takes thousands of people each year to see the Statue of Liberty. At night the glittering theatres around Broadway and Times Square are full of people going to see a musical.

Central Park

Contrasts – villages in Pakistan

Pakistan has an area three times larger than the United Kingdom and twice as many people. There are some big cities, such as Karachi, Islamabad and Lahore, but seven out of every ten people live in the countryside. Here they try to earn a living working on small farms.

A village in the Huntza valley, northern Pakistan

In the countryside houses are built from materials found locally. Houses in the north are built of wood and stone. In the south, houses are built from mud bricks, which are dried in the sun or baked in a kiln.

All village houses have flat roofs and few windows. This makes them cool in the long hot summers and easy to warm up during the winters. In the north of Pakistan it can get very cold in winter. Some houses have a courtyard or walled area outside where animals are kept.

There are normally one or two rooms. Electricity supply is rare, so people use candles and paraffin to provide light. Water usually has to be carried from a nearby water tap, pump or well. Cooking takes place over an open fire which burns wood or dried cow dung.

Inside a village house

Pakistan
- area: 800 000 square kilometres
- population: 120 million
- population in the countryside: about 80 million
- 4 out of every 10 people who work farm the land

People have to be more or less self sufficient and make or grow everything they need. The village blacksmith is very important. He makes and repairs tools used on the farms. The grocer sells things such as soap, tea, sugar and nuts which have been brought to the village from local towns. In larger villages there may be a watermill where local farmers can grind their wheat into flour. There may be a school for children to go to from about 7.30 in the morning until lunchtime. Some larger villages have small workshops where men and boys make things such as cloth or sandals to sell in the village or local market.

Village store in Pakistan

In the countryside, very few people have cars. To travel around, they use bicycles and mopeds. If people have a load to carry, they use carts drawn by horses, donkeys or bullocks. Many villages are linked to towns by brightly painted buses or minibuses. They are usually full to overflowing with people hanging on the sides or even sitting on the roofs.

Schoolboys on a crowded bus in Faisalabad, Pakistan

Contrasts – Rio de Janeiro

Rio de Janeiro is one of the largest and fastest growing cities in Brazil. It sprawls around and even up the sides of mountains and down to wide sandy beaches. Rio, as it is usually called, is home to about ten million people.

Copacabana, Rio de Janeiro

Rio's Sugar Loaf Mountain, just off the coast, rises 400 metres high above the sea. The city has a famous statue of Christ the Redeemer which stands high on top of Hunchback Mountain. But perhaps the most stunning thing about Rio is the gap between rich and poor.

To the south of the city are the wealthy neighbourhoods of Copacabana, Leblon and Ipanema. Here are luxury hotels, expensive apartments, restaurants, boutiques, art galleries and air-conditioned shopping malls. Rich and famous people come here from all over the world to watch Rio's famous carnivals.

The city centre has high rise apartments, banks and office blocks. There are also many beautiful buildings built over one hundred years ago.

Two of Rio's biggest favelas (hillside shanty towns) are Vidigal and Rocinha. They cling to the mountain slopes beyond Leblon. Over 80 000 people live in Rocinha. The houses were built quickly on empty land because of the housing shortage in Rio. Most of the houses have electricity and often they have running water but there is no sewage system. The favelas are often flooded and damaged by landslides during heavy summer rains. These poor areas are also centres of crime, and are dangerous to live in or visit.

Getting around in Rio can be difficult. Driving a car is only for the brave and traffic jams can occur at any time. Drivers do not often signal and pedestrians step off the pavements without warning. Finding a place to park is almost impossible. Buses are popular and used by everyone. They can be dangerous for tourists, as thieves try to steal their wallets as they pay their fare. Rio has a small, well maintained, safe underground railway system. It runs between the centre and Bofafogo, and is cheap and fast.

Rocinha, Rio de Janeiro

How it all began

The first settlements grew where they did for different reasons. Perhaps there was good soil for growing crops, which most families did. Maybe there was fresh water nearby, a wood for fuel and building materials. If the land had good views, it would have been easy to defend. Some places could offer more of these advantages than others, so at these places settlements grew.

When people grew more crops or bred more animals than they needed, they began to trade with each other. As people travelled in order to trade, a network of paths and cart tracks were made that joined villages together. The villages that were easier for people to reach got bigger. Some villages developed small markets which grew and grew.

Some settlements increased in size for other reasons. Sometimes it was because they were at a narrow point of the river which could be easily crossed by a bridge. Sometimes they were where a river was shallow and could be crossed by a ford, or in a valley or gap between mountains. If people wanted to move around they had to travel through these settlements. Shops, inns, stables and churches were built to serve the needs of travellers. Slowly some villages grew into towns.

Some settlements grew because they met a need people had for materials such as coal, tin, or lead. Others grew because the people who lived there were good at making things from iron, wool or cotton. Factories were built in these places, so people moved to work there, and these settlements grew.

In the eighteenth and nineteenth centuries, many settlements grew from small villages of a few hundred people to sprawling cities with populations of hundreds of thousands.

Early settlements

A thousand years ago the countryside was very different to what it is like today. Isolated farms and villages were dotted around the almost empty countryside. There were no large settlements.

One group of people to settle in Britain after the Romans left were the Anglo-Saxons, from Denmark and Germany. Settlers rowed up the rivers in the east looking for the best places to build their farms and villages. Their houses were rectangular in shape, windowless and built close together. Walls were built from split tree trunks or planks, and roofs were thatched. A hole was cut into the roof to let out smoke. Saxon homes were damp, dark, cold, smoky places. Around the village was usually a strong wooden fence or a wall to keep out wolves and unfriendly neighbours!

A village in the eleventh century

The Lord of the Manor lived outside the village. He owned all the village land, the woodland which he hunted in, and the stream. Villagers worked a number of strips of land scattered throughout three large fields. They paid rent to the Lord in the form of a tithe, which was part of their crops. Even when crops failed, the Lord had to be paid. The Lord of the Manor lived in a large stone house which was surrounded by a walled garden. The garden had orchards, bee hives, and space for vegetable plots.

William the Conqueror ordered a survey of all his lands in England so that he could collect taxes. He sent officials to every parish to record what land and property everyone owned and how much it was worth. They questioned the reeve, the man who looked after the Lord's land, and six peasants in each manor. They wrote everything down in the Domesday Book. The information in the Book gives us an idea of what life was like in eleventh century rural England.

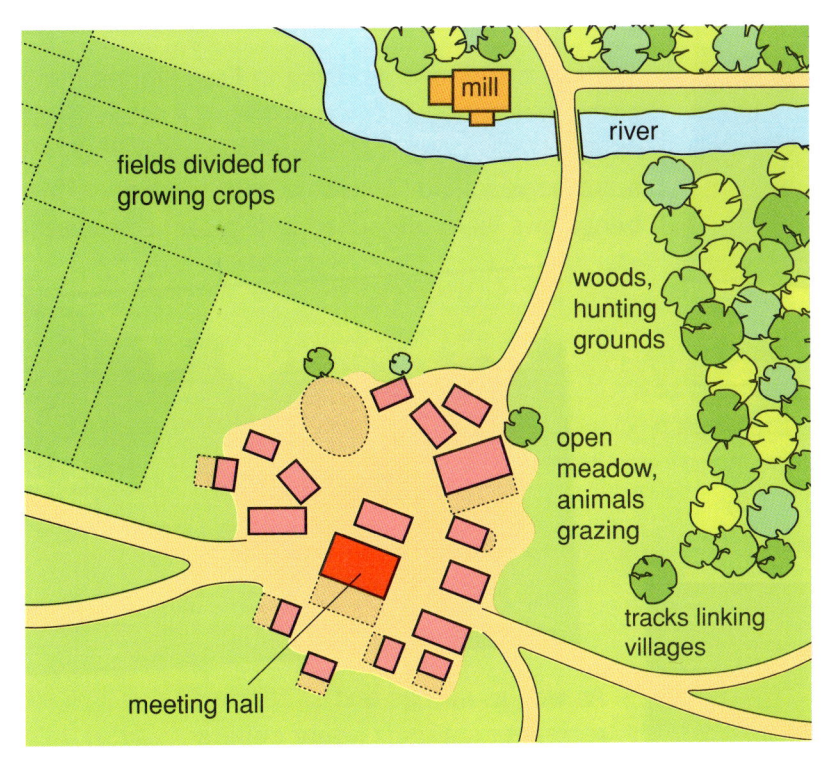

> 'Richard holds Birmingham from William. There is land for six ploughs, there is one plough in the demense. There are 5 villeins and 4 bordars and 2 ploughs. There is a wood half a mile long and 4 furlongs wide, and a mill. In the time of King Edward it was worth 20 shillings and it is still worth the same!'

Richard is Lord of the Manor. The Manor or parish has as much land as six teams of oxen can plough in one year and the Lord's land is about one-sixth of the total area. There are five serfs who are not free but subjects of the Lord, and four men who pay rent to the Lord for their houses. The woodland is about five hundred metres square. There is a watermill for grinding wheat into flour. It is worth about one pound.

Plan of the eleventh century village opposite

Place names

Place name endings tell us when a place received its name and what the countryside was like when settlers first arrived. Anglo-Saxon place name endings include:

-ing (territory of the people of)

-ton (hedged enclosure)

-wick (dairy farm)

-ley or -worth (clearing in a wood).

The Vikings, Romans and Celts named their settlements in the same way, using their own words.

East Morton

One way to see how settlements differ is to look at how the land is used. In villages there are more fields, woodland and open spaces than in towns. There are fewer factories, railways and roads. Some land, however, is used in much the same way as in towns.

There is a variety of housing in East Morton, ranging from small terraced cottages to large detached stone houses. Most houses in the village are over a hundred years old. Mixed up with them are newer bungalows, semi-detached and detached houses.

Although St Luke's church in East Morton has a small congregation, it is at the heart of village life. Local people decorate the church with flowers, and look after the churchyard by mowing the grass and keeping it tidy. There is also a chapel in the village.

As well as swings and slide, there is recreation ground, where children play football and cricket. On the edge of the village is a nine hole golf course.

One shop in the village sells newspapers and groceries. It is also a post office. There is a public house and a hairdressers. There is an antiques shop and a fish and chip shop but these are not open very often. Most people buy their groceries from nearby supermarkets.

The land in the village can be divided up and coloured in to make a land use map. It is easy to see what most of the land is used for. Fields, unused land and houses with gardens are important in East Morton. If a map like this was made for a town there would be many differences.

Key

- Houses and Gardens
- Shops
- Churches and Chapels
- Roads and Paths
- Water
- Woodland
- Farmland
- Industry
- Unused or Wasteland

Land use map of East Morton

East Morton First School is the only school in the village. About ninety children go to this school.

The village is surrounded by farmland. Most of it is grazing land for sheep and cattle. There is woodland and moorland close to the village.

The village hall or 'institute' is a place for local groups to meet and raise money through auctions, fairs and jumble sales.

Shops and shopping

Local shops, corner shops and village stores are handy as they can save a long journey to a supermarket if a bar of chocolate or a bottle of milk is all that is needed. They stock all kinds of things from cereals to shoe polish, vegetables and videos.

Inside and outside a corner shop

As these shops are small they cannot buy, store or display such a wide variety of goods as supermarkets can. This means that the price of the goods they sell is higher.

Local shops can be centres of the community, where people exchange news and views about local events as they shop. Many shops display information about things going on nearby, such as dances or jumble sales, and cards where people can display items for sale.

Few people living close to a corner shop or village store buy everything they need there. These shops are used for things needed urgently, daily, or forgotten in the weekly supermarket shop.

Over the last thirty years the car and the supermarket have completely changed the way we shop. Supermarkets need a lot of land for the store and car park, so they are built away from town centres, closer to where people live, and where land is cheaper. They buy in bulk, a lot at once, direct from the manufacturers so they get things cheaper. These savings are passed on to the customers.

Inside and outside a supermarket

Most supermarkets offer a wide variety of goods for shoppers to choose from. In addition to food, many sell clothes, toys, plants and even paint. In some supermarkets it is possible to cash cheques, send parcels, change the baby, and even have your photograph taken. It is true that there is, as an advertisement for one supermarket chain says 'everything you need under one roof!' Supermarkets have large car parks. Carrier bags full of shopping can be wheeled outside to a waiting car which is ready to take everything and everyone home.

A large supermarket

- sells over 20 000 different products to over 45 000 customers a week

- has nearly 60 000 customers in the week before Christmas

- employs about 400 staff

- is open for 78 hours a week

- has car parking for 1000 cars

- deals with approximately 3 lost children each week

Transport – too little

Until 1963 many villages were linked to nearby towns by railways. The railways had been losing a lot of money. The government felt that there were too many expensive railway engines, stations and workers, and too much track. In 1963 the government closed thousands of village railway stations and stopped many train services.

Steam engine at a village station in the 1960s

Trains were a cheap and easy way of travelling. Together with local buses, they acted as a lifeline for thousands of people in rural areas who had no transport of their own. The government cutbacks had a great effect on people who lived in the countryside.

Railways
- In 1960 there were 5000 railway stations and 33 000 kilometres of track.
- Today there are approximately 2472 stations and 16 500 kilometres of track.

Some station buildings were knocked down or left to decay. Others were sold and converted into homes, small factories or offices. Railway lines were taken away and the land returned to farmland or used as building land. The pieces of land are often used as footpaths and cycle ways.

This station building has been converted to a house.

There has been little has change to the railway network since the 1960s. A few railway stations have been rebuilt, usually in towns where it was felt there was a need for them. The services provided in villages, such as schools and shops, have declined as car ownership has increased. This has left people who have no transport of their own even more isolated. The only kind of public transport left for people to use are buses.

A few passengers on a village bus

758 / 754 / 746	MONDAY TO FRIDAY				
	758	754	746	754
Village Farm	0930	–	1430	–
Village Shop	0935	–	1435	–
Village Main Street	0943	–	1443	–
Village Long Street	0946	–	1446	–
Field End Lane	0955	–	1455	–
River End	1010	1310	–	1510
Long Lane East	1030	1330	–	1530
Big Town Square	1055	1355	–	1555

In rural areas the fares collected from passengers may not be enough to cover the cost of the fuel for the bus, let alone the wages of the driver. The bus company would make a loss on these routes if they did not receive grants from local councils, who see them as a vital link for people who live in villages. Even so, larger villages may have a service of only three or four buses a day and small villages none at all.

Young people, especially those who want to leave the village in the evening for the excitement of the town, can feel trapped. They have to rely on their parents or other people for lifts to local cinemas or discotheques. Most village households do have a car so they are not completely cut off. A car is essential for people wanting more than the village can provide.

Environmental change – villages

Over a hundred years ago, villages were farming communities and most people relied on farm work to give them a living. People rarely moved out of the village as they had little free time or money, and transport links were poor by today's standards.

As a result there were more shops, which sold a variety of things from food to household goods. There were lots of public houses, and perhaps most important of all, a blacksmith or 'smithy'. Here horse shoes were made and fitted, and household and farm equipment was made or mended. As farms began to use more machinery, there were fewer jobs. The population of many villages fell as people moved to the towns to find work.

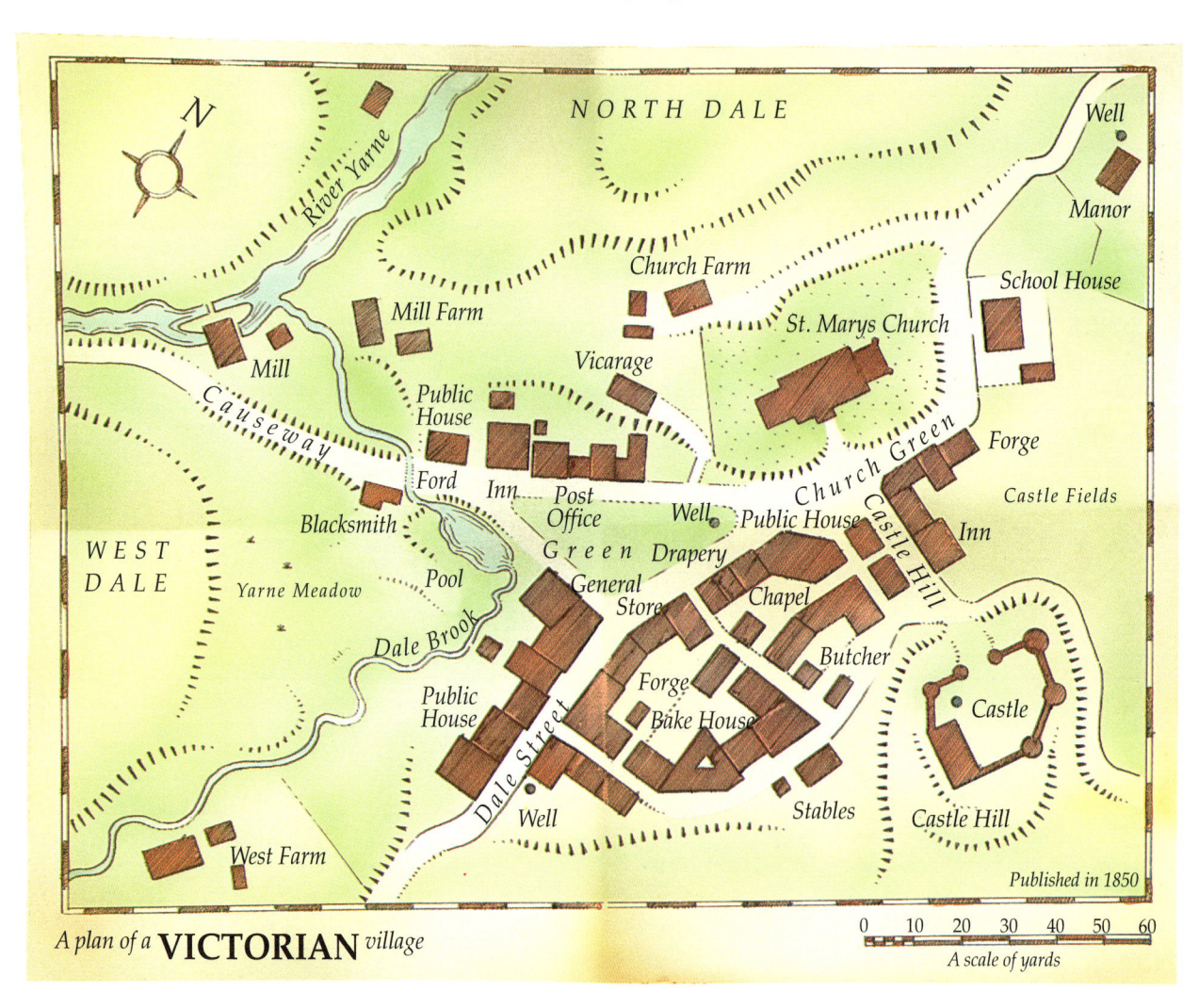

A plan of a **VICTORIAN** village

Published in 1850

0 10 20 30 40 50 60
A scale of yards

What differences do you imagine you would find in this village today? What new things might there be? How would the buildings have changed?

The car has made villages attractive places to live again. People can have the peace of village life and, if they use their car, all the advantages of a town.

Wealthy people, new to the village, have bought attractive houses and cottages and modernised them. Sometimes they live in them and sometimes they use them as weekend cottages. As a result, house prices have risen so much that often younger local people can no longer afford to live in the village they were born in.

This bottle kiln at West Hallam in Derbyshire has been renovated and converted to a craft centre with a shop and cafe.

Projects to make small areas of villages and towns cleaner and more attractive are widespread. Often volunteers, people who are unpaid, will clean, paint and plant corners of a neighbourhood that have become unwanted and vandalised over the years. Once finished, places cleaned up in this way become popular with people who want to sit and rest and enjoy the wildlife that soon comes to these green corners.

Land use in towns

Towns are busy, bustling places that provide services for people who live in or around them. Land in towns is in short supply so it must be used wisely. A lot of things have to fit into a small area.

Cupar town centre

To make sure that the land in town is used wisely, people who want to build houses or factories have to get permission from the council. The council will only give permission if they are sure that there is a need for the building and that it will not spoil the environment for everyone else.

The photograph shows a town centre. There are a lot of differences between this view and what you might expect to see in a village. There are fewer fields, areas of woodland and open spaces, and more factories, car parks and roads.

Sports centre

Industrial units

Car park

KEY

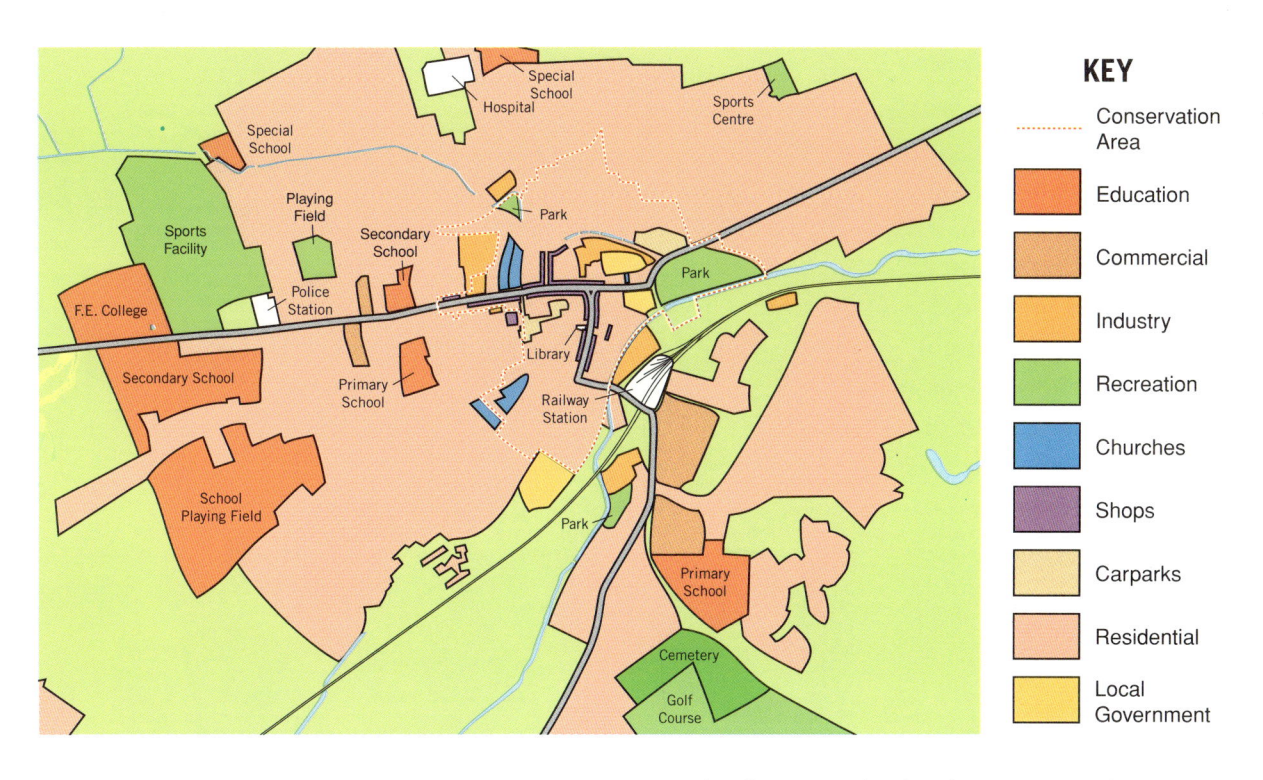

- Conservation Area
- Education
- Commercial
- Industry
- Recreation
- Churches
- Shops
- Carparks
- Residential
- Local Government

Church

Secondary school

Park

Busy roads

By looking at the land use map of Cupar it is easy to see what most land is used for. The small illustrations are of some of the land uses shown in the aerial photograph. Can you spot where they are? The captions will help.

Places change

Settlements are always changing, mostly in ways that we hardly notice. Perhaps someone is painting their house, building an extension or knocking down an old garage. The view might look much the same as it did a week, a month or even a year ago, but it is changing, slowly.

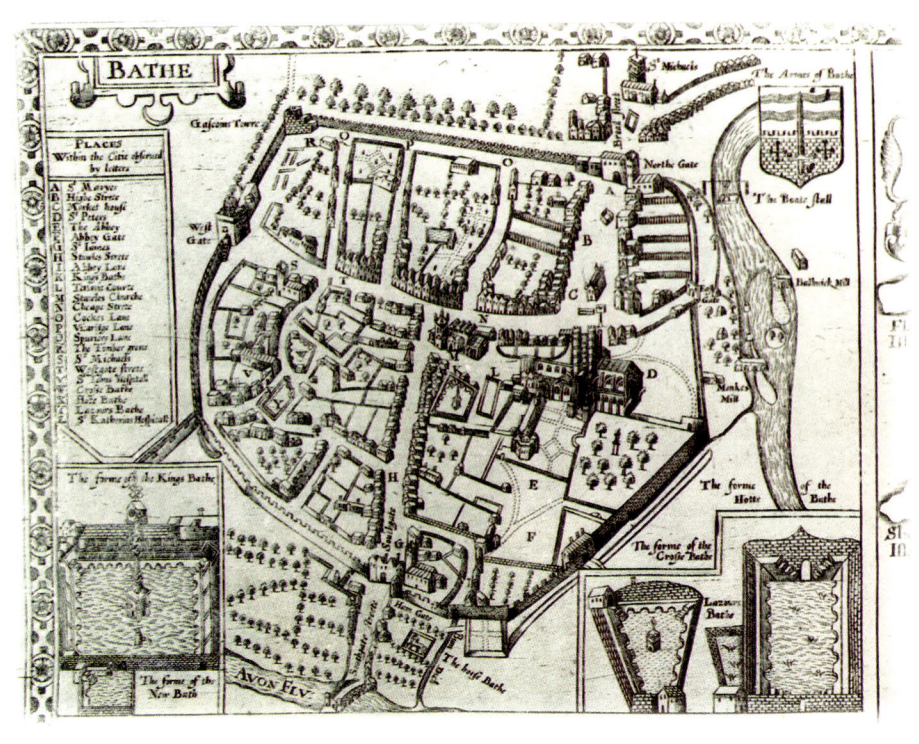

Seventeenth century picture map of Bath

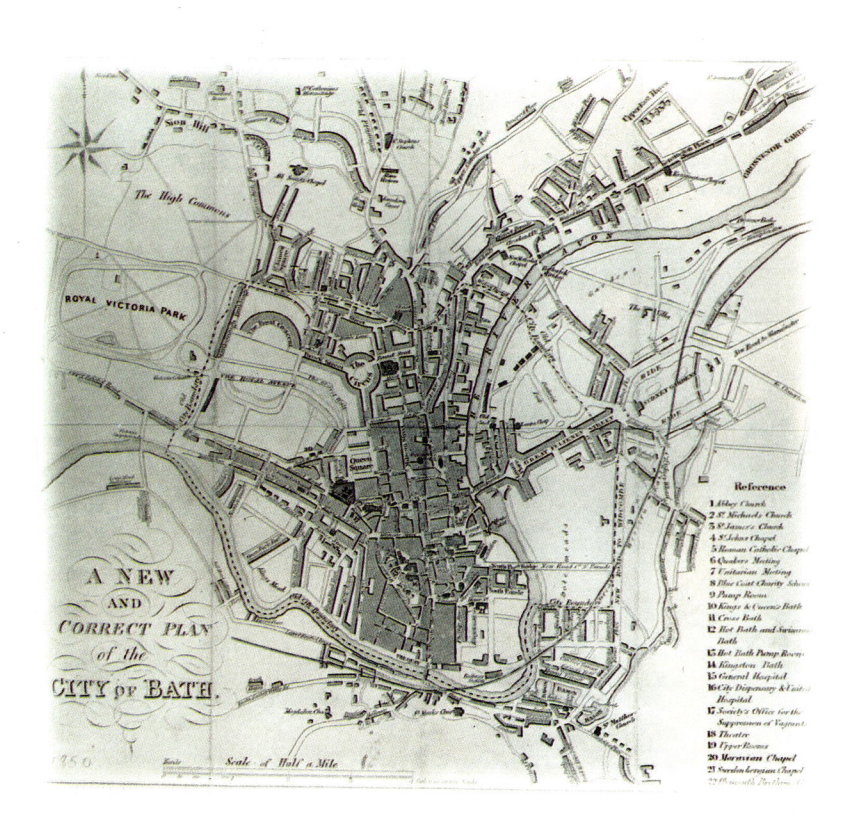

Sometimes settlements are changed quickly over just a few years. New housing estates, shopping malls where small shops used to be, or factory units with motorway link roads, covering green fields, can change the nature and character of settlements forever.

Victorian town map of Bath

Old photographs and maps can help tell the story of how a settlement has changed. Maps covering about a hundred years will show how a settlement has spread and developed. Photographs can show these changes, as well as differences in the way land is used, differences in buildings, transport, and how people dressed.

Ilkeston around 1910

Ilkeston in the 1990s

> Main Street had trams running along it and at the end was a tramshed. They've all gone now. The tramshed was where the entrance to the shopping centre is now.

One of the most interesting ways of collecting information about how a settlement has changed, and how the changes have affected people's lives, is to talk to parents and grandparents. Often they can remember lots of things that have changed in their lifetimes. They may remember what buildings were once used for, or where things used to be.

> The building in the corner which is a do-it-yourself superstore used to be a cinema. On Saturday afternoons we used to go down and watch James Cagney or Humphrey Bogart for sixpence.

Out-of-town shopping

Since the mid 1980s shopping centres have been built on the outskirts of towns and cities. Some of these centres have a few large stores such as do-it-yourself superstores, carpet and furniture warehouses.

More recently, out-of-town indoor shopping centres have been built. They are often on areas of land once used by factories or as waste tips, away from towns and cities. They are close to main roads and motorways so that customers can get to them easily and quickly from places far away. These centres are often home to hundreds of different shops.

The Metro Centre

The largest out-of-town shopping centre in Europe is the Metro Centre near Gateshead in north-east England. It was built on land where a power station and an ash tip once stood. It is just half an hour's drive away for two million people.

There are 340 shops, stores and kiosks in undercover, tree lined and air conditioned malls. If placed end to end, they would stretch for about four kilometres! In addition there are restaurants, a bowling alley, cinemas, discos and a hotel. The car park has spaces for 12 000 cars. Forming part of the centre is Metro Land, Europe's first undercover theme park. Up to 2500 children can have fun here while their parents shop.

The Metro Centre

- The Metro Centre has its own railway station which is used by about 500 000 people each year.
- Over 3 million bricks can be seen on the outside of the centre.
- On the inside, 1450 doors are the entrances to 340 stores.
- 27 air-conditioning units keep the air fresh.
- 67 closed circuit television cameras keep everyone safe.

Inside the Metro Centre

Centres like these are good news for shoppers, who can buy everything they need without walking too far or getting cold and wet. They can relax in one of the cafes or restaurants if they wish.

Not everyone has gained by these new ways of shopping. Many smaller shops in town and city centres have closed because of a lack of trade. Many shop owners have complained to local councils about the new centres taking their customers away. Some councils have tried to encourage people to come back by making town centres more attractive. They have paved streets, put in benches for people to sit on, planted trees and made gardens.

Revitalised city centre, Hemel Hempstead

Bypass

Many of our roads are choked with traffic, but lorries clanking through narrow streets are no longer the common sight it used to be. Over the years bypass roads have been built. These keep passing or 'through' traffic moving quickly along to other places, avoiding the narrow, often twisting, streets in the centres of many market towns.

Traffic in a narrow street

Vehicles and roads
- In the United Kingdom there are over 22 million vehicles scattered along a third of a million kilometres of road.
- 3000 kilometres of the roads are motorway.
- Motorways cost an average of £7 500 000 per kilometre to build.

Bypass roads can solve a lot of problems. They reduce congestion in town centres, by taking vehicles away. This means that there are fewer delays, safer roads, less air pollution and excess noise. Bypass roads have made towns more pleasant places to visit, but not everyone thinks that they are a good idea.

The A34 road will bypass the town of Newbury in Berkshire. It will link towns and cities to the north with the south coast and Channel ports such as Southampton and Portsmouth. It is estimated that 400 lorries an hour will be taken away from the town.

A lot of farmland and woodland will have to be cleared to make way for the new dual carriageway road. The road builders have to make sure that wildlife habitats are disturbed as little as possible. Over 200 bat boxes will be made, and badgers and dormice will be moved to safer places. Over 100 000 trees and new hedgerows will be planted to attract new wildlife and hide the road. To reduce noise, earth mounds will be made and planted with bushes, and the road will have a special asphalt surface.

Aerial view of land near Newbury showing the proposed route of the A34 in yellow

Newbury bypass protesters - tree people

Many people feel that the countryside with its ancient woodland is very important and should not be cleared for another new road. They believe that instead of building new roads, the government should look for ways to reduce the number of cars and lorries already on the roads. Some people want to stop the road being built. They protested by lying down in front of lorries and bulldozers. Some lived in the trees and would not come down, even when the road builders started to cut down trees nearby.

Journey through a city

Although no two towns or cities are the same, a journey from the outskirts to the centre will show similar patterns in the way that land is used. The same kinds of activities are grouped together.

A settlement may have grown for one main reason to begin with. Perhaps the castle offered people protection from robbers, or maybe there were reserves of coal or tin which people needed. In most towns, the reason why they began to grow has since disappeared or become unimportant.

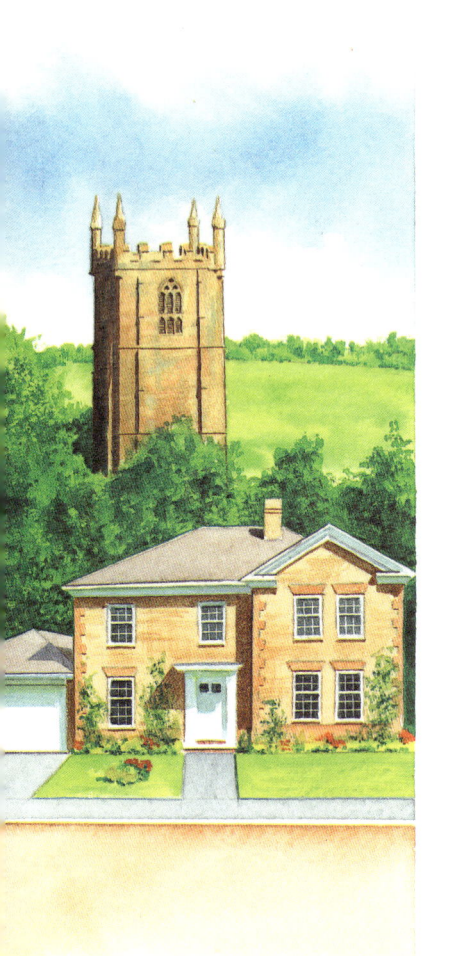

Commuter zone

The commuter zone is made up of small towns and villages around the city. The people who live there depend on the city itself for most things. Houses are in all shapes and sizes and usually have gardens. Some factory units have moved to towns in this zone.

Outer suburbs

The outer suburbs are on the edge of the city. Here are larger houses, built in Victorian or Edwardian times. There are also small estates of modern detached and semi-detached houses. Most have large gardens.

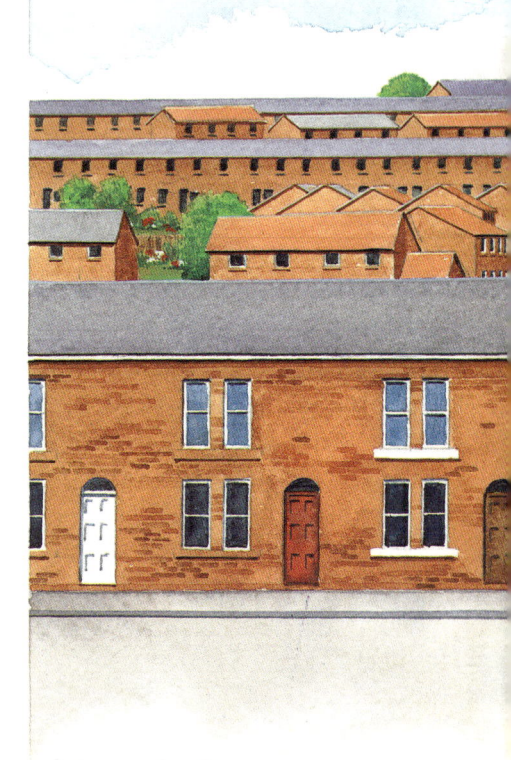

Inner suburbs

Houses have two or three bedrooms and are usually made of brick. Some are terraced houses built without bathrooms. A few large houses were built for wealthy people. There are also more modern housing estates from the 1950s and 60s built by local councils. Some houses have small gardens.

Nowadays towns grow for all sorts of different reasons. Usually they grow because they are places where jobs are found and people like to live quite close to where they work.

Twilight zone

This zone was once full of busy factories. Nowadays a lot of them are empty and falling down. In this zone there may also be canals, railways, warehouses and rows of small terraced houses that have small back yards but no gardens. Today some old warehouses are being converted into flats and offices.

City centre

The city centre is a busy place, full of people by day but empty at night, as very few people live there. There are shops, offices, hotels, cinemas and many other things that make the rest of the city work.

City centres

In the centres of old cities, shops and houses once stood together side by side in narrow twisting streets. Today the character of city centres is very different.

Manchester city centre

Street plan of the area in the photograph

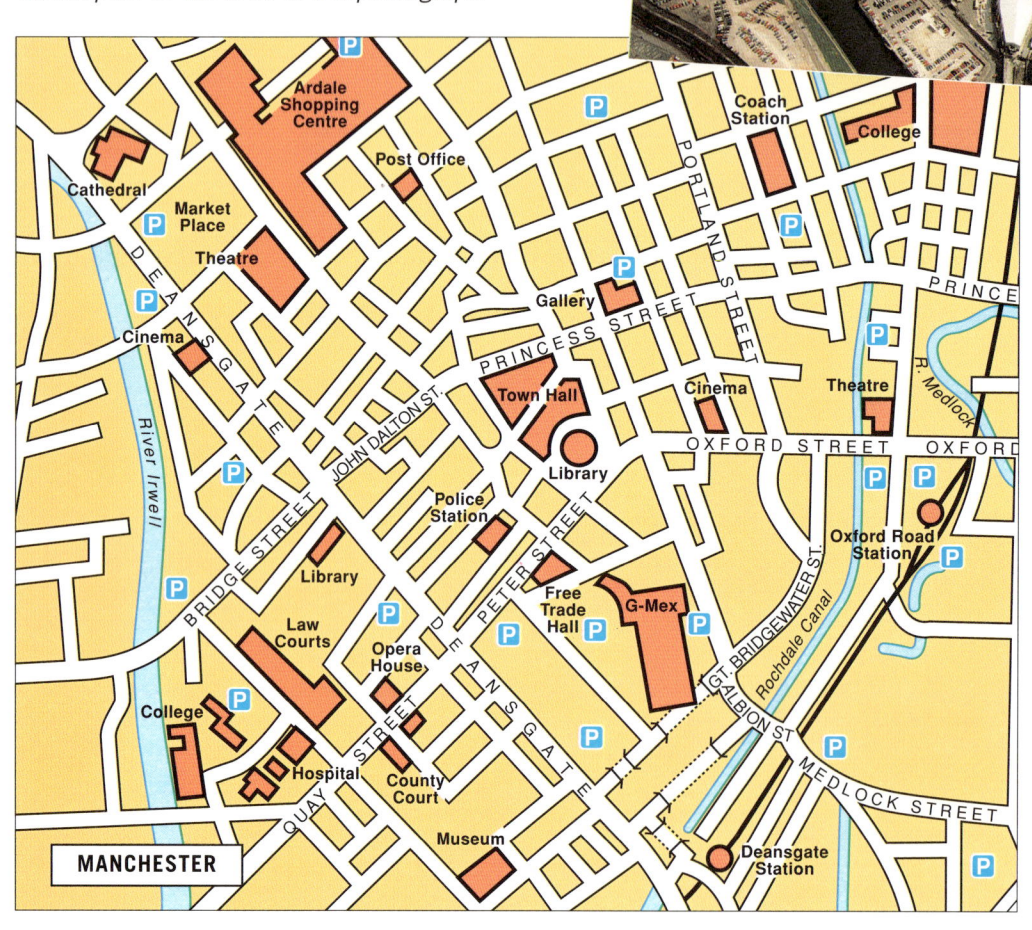

As the city centre is a place where most important roads and railways meet, it is easy for people to get to. Land is expensive to buy in city centres, so only large shops and offices can afford to be there. Buildings tend to be high in city centres, to make as much use as possible of the small amount of land available. This is noticeable in New York, Chicago and Hong Kong, which have the tallest city buildings in the world.

A lot of important buildings are found in city centres. They are often grouped together into small zones. Tourist guides and city maps are useful in helping to find these buildings.

Hotel zone
Hotels and restaurants are often close to railway stations and main roads.

Industrial zone
This is usually at the edge of the city centre. There are warehouses, factories, canals and railways.

Entertainment zone
This includes theatres, cinemas and ice rinks.

Educational zone
Here there are museums, art galleries, libraries, colleges, universities and hospitals.

Administrative zone
This zone has the town or city hall, a police station, law courts and government offices.

Houses in the United Kingdom

During the Second World War many homes near city centres were destroyed by bombs. Many others were almost a hundred years old and were cramped, poorly built and not fit to live in.

Many of these slums were condemned by councils who wanted to build new homes for people to live in. The price of land around city centres is high, so many councils decided to follow an American idea and build high rise blocks of flats. These were surrounded by grassed areas so that they were not too close to one another.

The high rise blocks were thought of as being the answer to all housing problems. However, they were not popular with the people who lived in them. The buildings did not look attractive and they were cheaply built. Lifts and corridors were often vandalised and young children could not easily play outside. Over recent years many high rise blocks have been modernised. Others have been demolished to make way for more traditional housing.

A tower block being demolished in Hackney, London

In some towns and cities new life has been breathed into old factory buildings and warehouses. Many have been redeveloped to make fashionable but expensive homes and apartments. Some of these have become very popular, especially those that overlook redeveloped dockland, canal basins or rivers.

Redeveloped dockland apartments and shops at the Albert Dock, Liverpool

Council housing estate in Keighley, West Yorkshire

Home owners who wish to improve or renovate their homes can ask their local council for a grant. The money is used to put in such things as new windows, doors, central heating, or to replace a worn roof or old electric wiring. The grants help to make houses more attractive as well as more comfortable to live in.

Over the last forty years, local councils have built housing estates on cheaper land further away from city centres. The small houses were cheaply built, but they sometimes had small gardens and play areas for children. It was possible for neighbours to talk to one another which did not happen in high rise apartments. Often hundreds of homes were built on one estate. Little thought was given to providing attractive places to walk or shop. Often there were few trees or garden areas, and there was little or nothing for young people to do.

Large houses are often built in developments on parcels of land on the outskirts of towns and cities. Often they are next to large Victorian houses. These new houses are well built, have gardens, garages and a range of fittings to make life comfortable.

A modern estate of large houses

Transport – too much

The places busiest with traffic are city centres and the main roads that lead to them. The roads are often congested (clogged with traffic), especially during the morning and evening rush hours, when people are travelling to or leaving work. Sometimes traffic comes to a complete standstill because there is so much of it. The same roads in the middle of the morning, afternoon or evening can be quite empty.

Traffic jam in smog, London

London was built largely before the car was invented. Each day about one million vehicles move around central London, at a speed which is rarely greater than 20 kilometres per hour.

Cities pay a price for all this traffic. Not only are there bunged up roads, angry motorists and pedestrians, but also noise, pollution, and more and more land being swallowed up by car parks.

Vehicle exhaust gases are poisonous. In some cities, like Tokyo and Athens, where pollution from vehicles can get very bad, policemen and pedestrians wear masks to protect themselves.

There are lots of ways to get into, out of, and around towns and cities. Different types of transport are used to do different jobs. Buses and taxis carry workers, shoppers and tourists to different parts of the city. Coaches, trains and aeroplanes can take people much further away.

Creating ways for cars and people to live together in towns and cities is not easy. Few cities have solved their traffic problems although many have made a start. Cities such as Oxford and York have park 'n' ride schemes, where motorists leave their cars in car parks on the edge of the city and take a bus to the centre. Some cities such as Newcastle and London have underground railway systems. Manchester has a new tram system. Many more cities have created bus lanes on their main roads. Cars are not allowed to travel in these at certain times of the day when traffic is busiest. In every city there are one way systems and traffic lights to keep traffic moving freely and safely.

44 Environmental change – cities

Sometimes environmental change in our towns and cities is swift and violent, perhaps because of a fire or an explosion. In other cities throughout the world, change through earthquakes can be devastating.

Bomb damage in London, World War II

Earthquake damage in Udine, northern Italy

London Docklands with Canary Wharf Tower

Docklands redevelopment scheme

- covers an area of 22 square kilometres
- contains 17 000 new homes
- includes almost 90 kilometres of waterfront around rivers and docks
- includes the Canary Wharf Tower - the United Kingdom's tallest building - which was built with 27 000 tonnes of steel and half a million bolts
- attracts nearly two million visitors a year

Most change in our towns and cities is planned.

One of the largest changes in a city is the development of London Docklands. In Victorian times trade was brisk in the Docklands area. The docks were full of ships taking goods made in Britain to places all over the world. There were factories, warehouses, and rows of houses for dockers and their families to live in.

Over the last fifty years, all the docks have closed. Thousands of jobs were lost, and the Docklands became very run down. In 1981 plans were made to give the area a new lease of life. New houses, shops, offices, restaurants and art galleries were built around Canary Wharf Tower which is almost 250 metres tall. The Docklands is now an attractive place for tourists to visit.

Sometimes buildings change their uses. Many churches and cinemas have been sold, as people do not use them any more. They are now used as bingo halls, shops, offices or even family homes.

Other buildings are completely new and reflect the changing nature of people in the United Kingdom. In the 1950s and 60s many people from India, Pakistan and the West Indies came to live and work here. They were keen to keep up the way of life they knew. Muslims from countries such as Pakistan built mosques, and Sikhs and Hindus from India built temples to pray in. These are increasingly common, especially in London and the industrial cities of the West Midlands and Northern England.

Conurbations

During the Industrial Revolution the population of the United Kingdom grew rapidly. In addition, lots of people moved to towns to work in the factories. Settlements got bigger and bigger. Eventually, settlements that were close together joined up. It became difficult to tell where one finished and another began – they formed a conurbation.

Often several settlements became joined up in this way as ribbons of houses were built alongside main roads. The farmland that once separated the settlements was covered by houses, factories, railway lines and roads. Villages nearby were swallowed up by the expanding towns and are now districts or areas within them.

A village grows into a conurbation

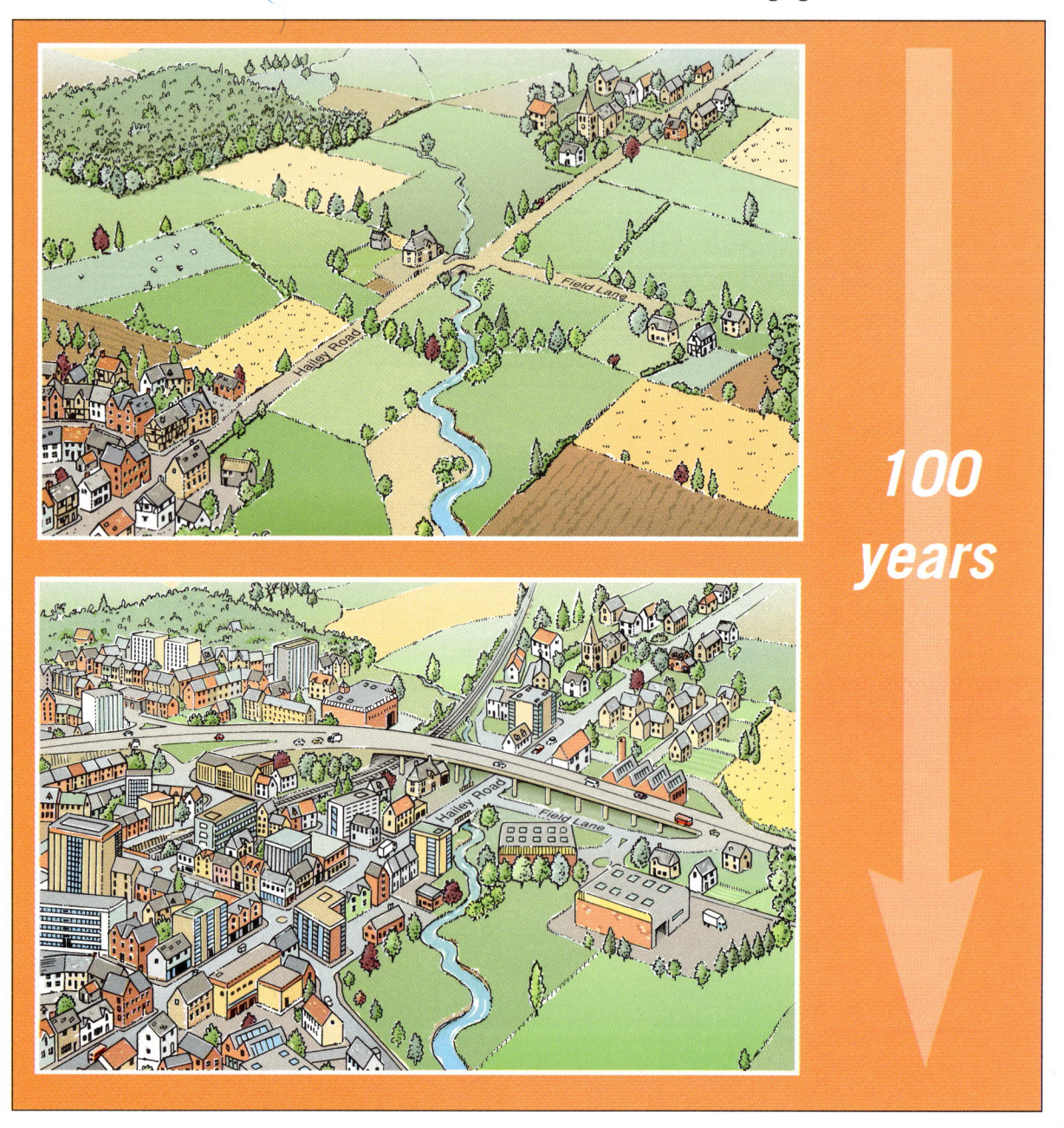

100 years

There are several conurbations, especially in the industrial areas of northern England and the West Midlands. Many of them have grown so much that planners have surrounded them with green belts to try to stop them from growing any more. Green belts are areas of open countryside where new building is banned unless the council gives special permission. People from the conurbations often go to the countryside to relax and enjoy themselves.

There are several large conurbations in the United Kingdom – the largest is Greater London. With a population of nearly eight million, Greater London is the third largest conurbation in Europe. It comes behind Paris in France and the Ruhr on the river Rhine in Germany.

Conurbations in the UK

The largest conurbations in the United Kingdom behind London

West Midlands	2 324 000	(Birmingham 992 800)
Greater Manchester	2 310 000	(Manchester 44 700)
Central Clydesdale	1 650 000	(Glasgow 689 200)
West Yorkshire	1 547 000	(Leeds 712 000, Bradford 468 800)
Tyneside	762 000	(Newcastle 277 800)
Belfast	441 000	(Belfast City 295 100)

Index

airports 7
apartments 14, 40, 41
art galleries 7, 14, 39, 45

bicycles 13
blacksmith 13, 26
bungalows 5, 21
buses 13, 15, 24, 25, 43

car parks 15, 23, 28, 32, 42, 43
cars 2, 3, 13, 23, 35
 in cities 15, 42-3
 and village life 25, 27
churches 6, 17, 20, 29, 45
cinemas 25, 37, 39, 45
cities 3, 4, 6-7, 8, 17
 centres 33, 36, 37, 38-9, 41, 42
 environmental changes 44-5
 New York 10-11, 38
 Rio de Janeiro 14-15
 traffic in 42-3
 travel through 36-7
colleges 7, 39
commuters 36
conurbations 46-7
cottages 4, 21, 27
countryside 12-13, 18, 24, 35, 47
crime 15
cycle ways 24

department stores 7

electricity 12, 15
entertainment 7, 39
 see also cinemas; theatres

factories 17, 20, 28, 32, 46

in cities 37, 39, 45
conversions 24, 40
units 30, 36
farming 12, 13, 26
farmland 20, 24, 35, 46
farms 4, 6, 12, 18, 26
flats 4, 37, 40

gardens 5, 8, 18, 21
 in cities 33, 36, 37, 41
green belt 47

hamlets 4, 6
holiday camps/villages 9
homes 4, 8-9, 18
hospitals 7, 8, 39
hotels 10, 14, 32, 37, 39
houses 4, 8, 28, 36, 46
 in cities 37, 38, 45
 detached 5, 21
 estates 30, 36, 41
 public 6, 20, 26
 semi-detached 5, 21, 36
 stone/thatched 18, 21
 terraced 4, 5, 36
 in United Kingdom 40-1
 village 12, 21, 27
 workers' 45

inns 17

land use 20, 28-9, 36-7
libraries 7, 39

markets 13
motorways 30, 32, 34
museums 7, 39

newspaper, local 7
noise 3, 34, 35, 42

offices 10, 14, 24, 37, 38, 45
open spaces 20, 28
overcrowding 8

parks 8, 11, 29, 32
police stations 7, 39
pollution 34, 42
post office 6, 20

railway stations 7, 24-5, 33, 39
railways 20, 24, 25, 46
 in cities 37, 38, 39
 underground 15, 43
recreation grounds 20
restaurants 11, 32, 33
 in cities 14, 39, 45
roads 20, 28, 30, 34-5
 in cities 10-11, 38, 39, 46
 main 32, 39, 42, 43, 46

schools 6, 7, 13, 21, 25, 29
settlements 4-5, 6-7, 8, 30-1
 early/first 16-17, 18-19
 growth of 36, 46
sewage system 15
shopping, out-of-town 32-3
shopping centres 31, 32
shopping malls 14, 30, 32
shops 7, 11, 17, 22-3, 25
 in cities 10, 37, 38, 45
 small 6, 30, 33
 village 13, 20, 22, 26
skyscrapers 10
slums 8, 40
suburbs 36
subways 11
supermarkets 7, 20, 22-3
superstores 31, 32

theatres 11, 39
tourism 15, 39, 43, 45
towns 2, 3, 4, 6, 7, 43
 centres 23, 28, 33, 34
 commuter 36
 environmental changes 27, 44
 expanding 46
 from villages 17
 hillside shanty 15
 land use in 20, 28-9, 36-7
 linked to villages 13
 market 34
 new 8
 out-of-town shopping 32
 railway stations in 25
traffic 15, 34, 42-3
trains 11, 24, 43
trams 31, 43
transport 24-5, 26, 31, 42-3

universities 7, 39

vandalism 27
village halls 6, 21
villages 3, 6, 8, 9, 16, 46
 commuter 36
 development of 17
 early 19
 East Morton 20-1
 environmental changes 26-7
 isolated 7, 18
 land use in 20-1
 in Pakistan 12-13
 transport links 24, 25

warehouses 32, 37, 39, 40, 45
waste tips 32
water 12, 15, 16

Published by BBC Educational Publishing
First published 1996
© John Corn / BBC Worldwide (through BBC Education) 1996
The moral right of the author has been asserted.

All rights reserved. No part of this publication may be reproduced, stored in any form or by any means mechanical, electronic, photocopying, recording or otherwise without the prior permission of the Publisher.

Paperback ISBN: 0 563 37506 X
Hardback ISBN: 0 563 37558 2

Colour reproduction by Dot Gradations, Essex
Cover origination in England by Tinsley Robor, London
Printed and bound by Cambus Litho, East Kilbride

Acknowledgements

With grateful thanks to Dale Frodsham, Fife Council; Brendan Quinlan, Hunting Aerofilms Ltd.

Illustrations: © Hardlines 1996 (pages 19, 21, 26, 29, 38, 46 and 47), © Steve Noon 1996 (pages 6/7, 16/17, 18, 22, 23 and 36/37), © Emma Whiting 1996 (pages 2, 3, 7, 28, 29, 39 and 43)

Photo credits: Arcaid / © Dennis Gilbert **p.4 (top right)**; Bath & North East Somerset Library and Archive Services (Bath Central Library **p.30 (bottom)**; Berwick Holiday Centre / British Holidays **p.9 (bottom)**; Butlin's Holiday Camps **p.9 (top)**; Canary Wharf Limited **p.45**; Collections **pp. 8 (top)** © Dorothy Burrows, (bottom) © Robert Deane, 24 (top), 304 © Brian Shuel; © John Corn **pp.20 (top left, middle, bottom), 21 (bottom), 41 (top)**; Dacorum Borough Council **p.33 (bottom)**; The Fotomas Index **p.30 (top)** © M.R. Gregory **p.27 (top)**; © Paul Harvey **pp. 27 (bottom), 31 (bottom)**; © Sarah Hooson **pp. 4 (top left, bottom), 5, 25, 41 (bottom)**; The Hulton Getty Picture Collection Ltd. **p.44 (top)**; Hunting Aerofilms Limited **pp. 28 (top), 35 (top), 38 (top)**; Courtesy Andrew Knighton **p.31 (top)**; Merseyside Development Corporation **p.40 (bottom)**; MetroCentre, Gateshead **pp.32, 33 (top)**; Mirror Syndication International **p.35 (bottom)** © Nick Turpin; Orient-Express Hotels **p.14**; Panos Pictures **pp 12 (top)** © Alain Le Garsmeur, (bottom) © John Miles, 13 (top) © Alain Le Garsmeur, (bottom) © Jimmy Holmes, 15 © Maria Luiza Carvalha; Tony Stone **pp. 10** © Jon Ortner, **11 (top)** © Ed Pritchard, (bottom) © Richard Elliott, **42**; Topham Picturepoint **pp. 24 (bottom), 40 (top), 44 (bottom)**; Woods of Bradford **20 (top right)**